THE YEAR OF OUR BEAUTIFUL EXILE

For my family,
in Mountain Standard Time

GASPEREAU PRESS · PRINTERS & PUBLISHERS · MMXV

The Year of Our Beautiful Exile

MONICA KIDD

For Alex – Pleasure to meet you at the Wayzgoose! Monica

And what is a year? [...] The whirl and roll of planets do not make a year a year, nor the breath of the trifling wind, changing from cold to hot, forming steam back into ice. Oceans of water that flow down from the tops of the Smokies and roll in the sea, they help some to make a year a year, but they don't make the year.

WOODY GUTHRIE, *HOUSE OF EARTH*

PRELUDE

So much lost this year and not, the
boy's small hands and triumphant
Yawp! Our sudden stops along the road
to pull focus. In this, the year
of our beautiful exile.

On Wilderness

CORRECTION LINE

The road sideslips with the
weight of the earth

curving.
And this is ordinary

as late crops, the tight fists of bales,
sun like a hand on skin.

Too few words, slamming shut.
The quick sideslip of eyes, a plot

twist.
This ordinary loss

and the way we go on.
The way that nothing

stays.

ON WILDERNESS

Wilderness. So overwritten it should probably
be granted a reprieve from definition.
— DON MCKAY

Plastic on the windows and a boxcar from Wisconsin.
The house next door, where everyone dies,
road signs honeycombed with bullet holes.
My footfall on the dirt road. The waist-high snow,
crisp in the March morning. Geese scrawled over the sky.
A net of numbers cast upon the country:
range roads, townships, pipelines, crossings.
These fallow fields. This quietude.

Here, wilderness is biblical.

SEASON OPENER

Islands emerge on the horizon,
seven skipped stones come to rest:
sisters, collared by lacy landwash,
aloof amongst the mountains of ice.
The *Ann Harvey* heaves and pitches,
sway-back in the Labrador Sea.

I have packed: sleeping bag, underwear, toothbrush.
Sixteen books sewn into the hems of my skirts,
a charm for melancholy and unwashed mouths.
The chopper roars and lifts away.

I imagined silence. Great towering cathedrals of silence,
silver in the ears and the pulsing of blood.
But send it through the prism and it is
wind and waves, small stones rolling,
birds growling deep in the earth,
my own heart smashing.

ST. ELMO'S FIRE

The camper arrives slung from a backhoe,
settles gently onto a pile of ash. A squirt of gas
and a match greets all that is left of my childhood:
how I lay on the bunk as my father drove, sheep
at the roadside, David Foster on loop, imagined lips
at my hairline, the future unfolding. The music
that launched me eastward, the muscle of it, my mast
pointed with blue flame, my compass spinning.

And now the compass spins again. Landlocked
and foundered, I am lost but for three small hearts
beating through the prairie night. I am struck dumb
as the fire burns, the sky pulsing with stars.

THE RICH IN AIRPORTS

In airports, the rich are unhurried, handled,
travel light. They have a sufficient,
but not excessive, number of pockets.

The rich do not cross their legs.
They are encouraged to ask questions.
Have accounted for delays.

The rich have been here before.
Are not offended by another's shoelace.
Never strain for the reading light.

The rich have flossed.
They wake wearing lipstick.
It does not stain the coffee mug.

The rich, with their perfect teeth
and mannered handbags,
do not fool us.

SYNAPSE

I arrive at the station, divine the four directions,
surface. A line of yellow cabs paws at the curb
as the world-weary churn through the chute and
wheel out into the night.

                                        A driver catches my eye,
and something in me—a twitch of the brow, a
clench of the fist—he is out of his car and
wading my way:

You have a sad face,
but a beautiful smile.

OSTINATO

Room service came with a table, an orchid,
a white-gloved waiter. The baby, whom I
walked and walked, our humped reflection
in the mirror at each turn, finally asleep, tucked
like a parrot under the heavy hotel blanket.

The water caught my eye. This pool before
the setting sun, the ships, the river and its seashells.
These swimmers, their industry, glints of light.
I pause. Freeze into the diorama of this baby and that,
a missing toothbrush, a flower, the black night. Ripples.

Long after the swimmers are gone, the water
remembers, slapping and slapping against
the walls of the pool, forever going nowhere.

DIRGE FOR A FELLOW TRAVELLER

You peeked at me from under the covers,
my back turned to Ottawa and that flag
frittering against the sky. A capital mourning.

A dot of tomato sauce, date stamped
two weeks in the past, is all that remains
of your solitary meal. The delivery charge,

and everything that followed.
Your name, this window, this bed.
Your life, half-masted.

A MAKESHIFT MARTINI SHAKER

It requires an attitude of the wrist.
A flick of the hair, the bearing of Buster Keaton,
a love for the way white layers on white,
the way a word can be both sour and sweet
when served with a boar's head.
The way nothing is ever
quite what it seems.

An emphatic *pumpf* as the line cook peeps
out the porthole of a door that swings
both ways. Feet like water on
flagstones in old Montreal.

AFTERMATH: NYC

One minus one. A son loses a mother, becomes what remains.
Black Irish taffeta rustling in my chest as I skitter to Studio 54,

all open thighs & big brass, the tick-tock of hips, the emcee and his
seductive buttons, the baby that will not change a thing, that brick

through the window, and, how, when the curtain rises and the
music throbs, the orchestra gone, how their absence

stops traffic. How we all die when the lights go down.
How there are no words. How silence is a fiction.

The blood in my ears, deafening. These are the weights
and measures of loss, and of what remains.

Deluge

STORM

Thunder last night, the kids and their lightening in the sheets, the fridge, all the dark corners of their minds lit up: the snap of one charge toward another. Now, the house quiet, and their absence pulled taut, I pace, restless as a dog. The water rises.

SOLACE

Everywhere you look, the names of banks and oil and oil chasers written over the sky. Nowhere to hide. But tonight the buildings are empty and dark. Muddy water laps at their footings. Across the swollen river, rusty remnants of the war memorial peep above the flood waters. All sunk, save for the word *Solace*. Soldiers' names sinking again into the black.

MENISCUS

Was like it for days. The river running fast and high, lopping at the banks. Spilling through the low places, threatening the loafers of the passersby who deftly swerved and saved their lattes. As though it hadn't happened. Heavy artillery beavering, even before the rain clouds passed.

ARBOREUS

Took you by surprise, the way it stood there, propped against the bridge like it had sprouted in the shoal and grown to height. People crossing the bridge would rest in its momentary shade, leaves rippling in the breeze, undisturbed by the ravelling predicament. Weeks passed as it flowered and fruited, walkers plucking apples on their sneaker shuffle home.

IT WAS LIKE THEY RESURRECTED THE TITANIC

An evacuation the size of Amsterdam but no reason not to golf. Come hell or high water, *yadda yadda*. You've got to spend your way out of a depression, and this city could use a little retail therapy. Cocktails, and the lovely music of the choppers overhead. Firefighters smiling, the strong set to their jaws.

DANGLE

Bodies appeared in the strangest of places in the days that followed. Draped over railings, suspended in cages over the roiling water. A power pole dangling from a crane like a giant crucifix twirling on a gossamer thread.

A NEW COURSE

Nobody thought about the fish. Stranded in parking lots, ball diamonds, soccer pitches. In basements. Backhoe buckets. A kitchen sink. A toilet bowl, severed from its gasket. An overturned bass drum. A firepit. The trunk of a Toyota Tercel. A little red wagon. A large black boot. A bassinet. A toy box. A suitcase. A child's wading pool. A tire swing. Concerned officials and willing children picked them up and rinsed them off, launching them down their raw new limnographies.

AFTERSHOCK

The heat that followed like a husband's hot breath, a thick, wet cloth that stopped up the nose and mouth. Phone lines went dead. Cotton from the trees spontaneously combusted. Drove the street cats wild, their whining in the failing light the sound of ill-loved children thrashing in their fitful sleep.

GHOST

In the great reveal as the water receded, gravity became
a wobbly table. The water changed. The light changed.
History popped its lid. In the café, a dead girl passed
carrying an empty coffee cup, her long skirt shushing over
the plank floor. I saw her face clearly.

MUG SHOT

Dorothy's slides were in the basement when the water came knocking. Floated the carousels right up out of their boxes so that the cat could hop from one to another, like pans of ice, all the way to the freedom of an open window.

When the water receded, the slides lay in a sopping heap, their Kodachrome colours blurred together like a mug shot of the vanished current. History swirled. Sons came before daughters. Altars stood bereft of lovers. Peonies stranded in the snow.

SHAKESPEARE

Summoning his inner bard, the mayor put out a call for nouns to describe on national television those who would walk the banks of the river in flood. (Later, a clause was enacted allowing the substitution of compelling descriptors.) Diaper licker. Hammer sack. Buzzard briner. Sharp as a heap of sawdust. Quick as a set of square tires. Cousin lover. Lost as a drunken cherry. Jug plucker. Cow tipper. This, of course, was many weeks after His Worship sat beside me at a play about Will being slaughtered by zombies. And that, gentle reader, is as true a story as they come.

RAINING CATS

They say there's a cat for every cowboy, and this was never more true than in High River, which is a town that lived up to its name. There were a lot of cats, and they all needed somewhere to go. So someone backed in a semi and loaded up six hundred of the furry little bastards. Crawling over each other, meyowling for their favourite pillows and catnip.

JUST LISTED

Don't look too bad, huffs Bobby Bare Chest, man-boy centaur, to his knock-kneed girlfriend. *Streets are a bit muddy, that's all.* This, as a small house fronting Memorial sprouts a *For Sale* sign, the occupants gingerly drying out their father's war medals, airing out the communion dress.

ON THE MISSING LINK BETWEEN ELECTRICAL STORMS AND PAYING IT FORWARD

For a whole week afterwards, there were thunderstorms of such intensity that the dog burrowed three feet into the basement floor. The kids wore sunglasses to bed. One dark night, my husband leapt out of the sheets, thinking—inexplicably—that our son had tipped over the refrigerator.

Strangely, the same week saw a rash of coffee Quixotes, people buying double-doubles for the next several hundred strangers to walk through the door of Timmy Ho's. For a moment in time, kindness—and earplugs—nudged the squiggle of Alberta's GDP.

Intertriginous

Poems for Evolution

Nature cares nothing for appearances, except in so far as they are useful

Squalor.

The word appeared like a bubble on his lips as he looked about at the ceiling hung with ribbons of negatives, a tin coyote, a devil's purse. The kitchen a crucible: fruit, seeds, nuts and bolts, anything at all might be baked into a loaf and served on a china plate with a nice Chianti and the morning's spinach. Fox Island hunkering in the cove, the wind bending the lupines double and smudging the grass to sable. This storied perch.

Squall, or. Like a sharp wind had blown clear through.

The beetles in Madeira lie much concealed until the wind lulls and the sun shines

Of evolution and what it said about God, geneticist J.B.S. Haldane remarked, *He must have an inordinate fondness for beetles.* For remove the soil, the houses and asphalt, the fighter planes and pop cans, the bed sheets; remove the entire residue of man, and the earth would remain, a husk of twitching bug feet. Set your mind to counting and come back when you are old, and still the number would not be great enough to hold them.

Throw up a handful of feathers, and all fall to the ground according to definite laws; but how simple is the problem where each shall fall

We are driving down a gravel road, faces prickly from the wind and sun, alders dusty in that way that brings back summer on the prairies, when time digs in its heels and fails to budge: I am eight or I am fifteen, all green bikini and bare feet on the back deck, too hot, with too many hours to fill before a breeze descends and the coyotes call. The sting of leather in a laced glove. The sun like a knife. The train coming and me singing *C-N-C-N-C-N* as the boxcars pass, straining for the music of distance. Dust like hot chalk, the air cracking. A dream that recedes with the telling.

Savages now sometimes cross their dogs with wild canine animals to improve the breed, and they formerly did so, as is attested by passages in Pliny

Nick was a boatman in Antarctica. Sailed to the islands one year and left the next, wondered what in hell had transpired that all the men wore long hair and beads. All those months growing thin and cagey in the land of ice, smoking for the company in it. Spoke like words were bags of water drooping between his fingers, unpracticed at time cards and newspapers. A horizon man.

There was a time, he said, *when a person showed up on South Georgia and was handed the keys to a dog team. First job was to trust them; second job was not to die.* The dogs made it easy. They knew the ice better than anyone and not a few of them perished in place of their drivers when a false turn led them over the edge and into a crevasse. All that changed when the snow machines came. Their noise, their belching blue.

To watch that man handle a dog —. Heave them onto his shoulders like blushing brides, their blue eyes flashing joy at the midnight sun. It could break your heart. Could make you want for the bottom of the earth.

We may console ourselves with the full belief that the war of nature is not incessant, that no fear is felt, that death is generally prompt

It ended badly. Dialing up my inner Brontë,
I swept downtown in the morning fog.
Pinned a note to the workshop door
and limped away, nothing more. And now:
The Earl's Chair comes see-sawing out of the past,
a reel in my heart for all the missing years.
For his face in sleep and his fingers forever teasing
the raw edges of things. Worse than dead

for at least the dead tidy up. Remember a dream:
something about whitewashed walls and a house
with infinite rooms. This too, you will forget.
But the dream does not forget the dream.
Evolution is this: to know a thing
and be ever so slightly changed by it.

Nothing is easier than to admit in words the truth of the universal struggle for life, or more difficult than constantly to bear this conclusion in mind

Sun on skin, we lizard in this clearing, two cups of coffee and an orange between us. It's something I read once, that love is sharing an orange, and so we do, popping the sections into our mouths, into the dark places between words. Speaking, retreating. Fingering the final piece and worrying it down to skin, cells. These shriveling jewels.

The crumpled sheet, the family weeping. The report. The way it marked before and after. The way I couldn't speak, won't speak. The ways we overflow with loss. That spruce with the double crown split like a tongue, what would it say? This is the hopscotch of love: cast a word, close your eyes, leap.

We behold the face of nature bright with gladness

The child sleeps, her weary head nodding at my breastbone. I am her vessel again, and she a tiny sailor, the points of our compass drawn in cursive. *Of the men he made to stand under the sky, they are as much what they are as what they are not*, he said, though I am paraphrasing. I think of this as we round the end of the lake and there, in the crook of the trail, is an aspen glittering in a small wind, volume translated into light, imperfectly, the way the world is captured by language: dots and dashes across leagues of thirsty ocean and creaking timber. Hold a leaf to her cheek and show her we are no different, all reticulations and bursting flesh.

Let us now consider the steps by which domestic races have been produced

Dear Mother—
My little garden has begun to sprout:
the stubborn potatoes, stiff as history, and
the beets, wall-eyed, escaping rank.
The tomatoes flooze from their pots,
their woodsy smell settling somewhere
behind my ribcage, small green fists of sky.
I push my hands through the soil like hair.

The tangled bank. The body electric.
What is a garden but a republic of poppies,
or a string tied to a young girl's finger?
I have learned to weed while the baby sleeps.
I have found that love will grow
amidst the shattered crockery.

So it is that the great Tree of Life fills with its dead and broken branches the crust of the earth

Margie cut my muslin and asked me again how much I wanted. *I'm tired of getting robbed,* I say to her, and she harrumphs. No light in her face, now that I look at her, her breasts pointing this way and that, but she's a fine hand with a pair of shears. *My own fault,* I say, not believing it. *I want to leave a note in the glove box for whoever goes through it night after night:* You're a prick.

Margie cut my muslin and charged me six yards instead of seven.

Not one of our domestic animals can be named which has not in some country drooping ears, and the view has been suggested that the drooping is due to the disuse of the muscles of the ear, from the animals being seldom much alarmed

The sky has opened
and the earth is torn.
Click goes the gun,
the camera—stop:

one, Mississippi
two, Mississippi

*

A shudder of thunder
and the blankness rings
when you stop

to listen.

Boom boom boom
go the drums.

When I view all beings not as special creations but as lineal descendants, they seem to me to become ennobled

A life spent in the lap of Nurture.
No deed to claim, she grew to fill the space
between two hands, spun from black loam and
of the place by luck. True, yet what is luck

but a bold misstep, a broken descender?
The words we choose are an alphabet of loss
or hope, depending on the weather. And now
these faces, their pleasing infant synchrony.

Black crow patrols the woods on taffeta wings,
its busy *shush-shush*; dog bursts after a spectre.
We are home here for as long as we are. The babies:
touch their puzzling heads, cool as buttercups.

Other Kinds of Hungers

how we die without appetite
and the way we live with hungers
that consume our hearts like another kind of dying

RICHARD BERLIN

BUFFALO JUMP

Here, in the land of rocks and empty sand,
the river tugs lazily at its long johns.
Turkey vultures skulk in their ominous capes,
bones lie belly up to the sun.

She presided here as a girl
chasing horses and little feet.
Sixty years later, a husband
gone, and a daughter, and still
the plaintive smile of the sky.

She became weightless with time.
Her bird's legs gobbled the cliffs
and her mind grew ravenous for Latin.
We went to her as children would, hoping,
as if walking were a prayer.

Until a little bomb dropped
in the vault of her skull,
left her in a chair
in a room, in a house.

The wind paces
just outside the window.

MR. X'S MIRACLE

He was weeks on that bed,
gnarled as an old fence post,
and just as still.
His sons wore ruts in the hallway,
guarded him with bared teeth.

Then:

Stick out your tongue, Mr. X.

And his jaw creaked open
like it needed oil,
and his tongue was a flash of pink,
moist, human—a hungry boy
hiding in the wreckage.

A small thing:
water, wine,
and many little fishes.

A VERY FORGIVING ORGAN

Still as a tree she stands,
hand to phone, phone to cheek.
A dusty diorama, the jackhammers muttering
as they will on a Tuesday. She's crying,
frozen in grief and the bare fact of January.
The dog and I, we keep our heads down,
slip our simple lives under our skirts and try to pass.

She stops us. Looks at me with a blackened eye
and down at the puppy, who stares back, cocks her head.
The girl kneels down, strokes the sleek black head and says,

in disbelief—*She's so happy.*

SALVAGE REGIME

October 1979.
The air smoldering with harvest,
your new Hush Puppies
still stiff from the box.
You learned to chase
your dutiful pencil around
the letters, crossing invisible borders
between one and the next.

A word.
laythepinkeraser
Another word.

It's those spaces I think of now.
How they filled with things
too sharp to say.

ACHILLES

A
body
made
invulnerable
save
for
one
forgotten
place.
Here's
where the
master
carves his
name.

FALLEN

It was sixty years ago,
that shot to the thigh.
Hauled from the slime
and stench to join the ranks of
wounded—more of them dead
from the slow suck of time
than from bullets.

He walked again.
Came home to a girl
he made his wife:
four kids, the mortgage,
a whole blessed lifetime.

In the end, the poultice cracked
and the years spilled through.

The Germans got him.
It just took them awhile.

HOW TO WASH A BODY AFTER DEATH

A tender dance, this slipping of fingers
through fingers, knuckles on cold flesh,
grace that is a copper penny passed
from palm to palm.

Rain against the window,
dogs howling at the black,
black sky. The end of days.

Coming Home

ON QUITTING MY JOB, AGAIN

In the bloodless light of 3 AM
my fears come to roost—

the baby's breathing
the metastasizing deadlines
the exact location of my soul

—casting their grotesque shadows
over the snowy ground, the sky slate-grey
the stars, all a-twinkle.

We orbit one another: mother to child,
child to mother, man and woman,
to couch, to floor, minutes chasing
the hour. I draft my resignation,
give it godspeed, letting it fall
into the empty night.

RUNNING ERRANDS

after Jan Zwicky

Turning that corner, no warning,
my face in the window, scowling
at the 8:47 sun, the bleating ads,
lizard brain grumbling and feet
slap-slapping to drag a plastic
wagon, which is the best thing
to happen to me in a month:

I am not beautiful. Not ugly.
Just inert as a worn board,
bracing.

I MARRY MY HUSBAND'S SMART PHONE

It always knows the right song to sing.
It remembers my birthday with a cheery *tra-la.*
Patient as Buddha, it is ever present, ever ready
for my word, a picture, a passing thought.
Without judgment, it receives my stumble forward
and recharges anywhere: coffee shop, kitchen table.
All the waiting places of our lives.

WHEN IN DOUBT, SET IT IN CASLON

> *Monica: Cu = copper = ½ pt. thick. Br = brass = 1 pt. thick.* VERY *handy for tightening up a loose line, two pt. leads make good thin spaces, but at some critical point you end up using snippets of cereal boxes, unwanted invoices and old X-ray film (and good sharp scissors) to flesh out lines. Onward!*
>
> EMAIL FROM DAVE CHURCHMAN

I squint: letters like shot across the page,
Ringwalt's motet screaming in my hindbrain.
I lean over garbage cans and broken drawers,
wrestle aphasia and my son's sticky fingers
to put words to page. Too dark in here.
Too messy. Too much, and not enough, and
there was a day when I could hear music
and stop time. But time is a bastard. And so are
these quoins and reglets, quads and points.
Nothing looks right, nothing ever looks right,
and why am I forever groping for new alphabets?
My knee-high daughter, minding her *p*s and *q*s,
correctly distinguishes *d*s from *b*s, while at forty,
I am still befuddled by Rs and 2s. Where's the justice?
These words we choose. How they elude us.

BADLANDS

> *... I experience a shudder of happiness at this.*
> *It is true, I thought. I am living a life.*
> PATRICK DEWITT

There is a log cabin in the campground I'd like to see and we wonder if it is new made to look old, truly old and moved here, or old *in situ*. I say yes, they could have retrofitted it with windows. Then, to the baby, whose face is full of pablum, I say: *They didn't have windows then. Only oilcloth. So dark. I would have made it two days then. How did they have babies in that? How did everyone not die of infection? I guess they did. The power of sanitation and infrastructure and vaccinations: so much greater than our jogging and our antidepressants and our organic food. But then all of their food was organic. They didn't have any pesticides because there hadn't been any industrial wars yet, no sarin gas, no napalm. Because pesticides are just another form of warfare, and nobody ever wins a war.*

And I stop. I look out the window at last night's rabbit and the thrush and the wolf willow heavy with their load of red berries, at the sun coming up over the badlands, at last morning's rain, the grimy streaks where my son has pawed the windows, and my husband, hungover from a night dreaming of work, and all of our wars, and the boy, desperate to be near him, and the dog, wet and morose from a year of neglect—I survey the ruins and the possibility—and the words are right there in front of and all around me: Nobody ever wins a war.

SPRING CLEANING

Tie a ribbon round the resignation letters,
box the crates of rejections with the body cast,
stiff and medieval and smugly Kahloesque.

Leave the bankers' boxes in the drip line.
Ball up the sticky notes and pack them
in your cheeks for the next nuclear winter.

Shred the divorce papers, the mortgages,
the water-stained receipts. Open the windows
and let the wind blow through.

Stop at the stairs by her meaty fist, an age since you
circled it in yours. Pin the flower behind her ear.
The days are long, but the years longer still.

HOW THE BODY REMEMBERS JOY

How you snug my hip with
two girls curled into sleep, my heart
humming an old tune it once heard,
a hundred times, the heat of a body
on a sofa never closer than brass strings
strummed against the night,
prowling at the windows.

My new love affair with F#:
the way it sits cock-eared
in the drum of my chest,
its sound of feet on earth, of quiet
rooms and a blank page, turning.

How the body remembers joy.
How the clocks stop.

FIVE-STRAND CHALLAH

Pinch and roll, pinch and roll. Dough resists the hand,
but let it rest. Listen while the years unspool.
Oh, constant companion, this urge for more
like butter on the tongue, and salt.
Quiet Sunday mornings and late nights, alone,
that which neither spoils nor decays, a heart
lifted by easy wins and muscled for the race.

The dough, rested, yields. Five strands:
you, me, her, him, her.
                    Here. Winding
and unwinding in equal measure.
Watch it Rapunzel on the borrowed bench.
This, too, the dominion of love.

SELFIE

Two girls, toes busy on the windowsill,
all cheekbones and kneecaps, discuss:

how illness abandons, the borderlands of love,
her ears hungry for small truths. From our perch

we watch the breathing of the black water,
up and down, fish in the air, the silver sky.

Her mind sketching bloodlines, heartlines.
How the rain collects here, where I was born,

its tunnels and alleys, her sandaled feet slip-slapping,
her scrutiny, her beauty, words flickering to life

as she learns the way home.

PALETTE

I am stopped. My flat shoes too fey for the slick rock whetted
by the sudden rage of thunder. These hills want teeth.
I double back. Cross the river, cream-in-coffee with the rain,

and walk until my feet find gravel that leads me up and up,
through sagebrush grottos and into sandstone hills sliced and
sluiced by deep Don McKay time. The sky towering

and these floozy hoodoos, our painted ladies hipped
against the feathery hills. I remember my mother,
watching me tie back my yellow hair, my eyes a shade

of swamp water, my wardrobe olive, drab.
Fearing the dust in my heart, she snapped:
Why won't you ever wear some colour? Downpours

and sentences raining, the day suddenly wild. I freeze.
A doe and two fawns, gangly and spotted. Three faces
turned to mine and mine to theirs, staring as our ears

fill with bugsong. I come in peace, I think at them.
But the fawns finish their mouthfuls and tiptoe away.
The mother and I stare for a hundred years

as coyote calls spill down the valley
and we give a little shudder for our children,
how we will fail them and how they will leave us.

But pray before they do they fill their palettes
with umber and myrtle and persimmon. Find beauty
in desolation, these colours of home.

RIPPLES

The house neatly folded and tucked away, I drive my three sleeping kids across the prairies, radio on, sloughs still and laced like fingers through the long hair of the cattails, the fields bleached, the crops done, the gardens plowed. The hum of the wheels and analog scratch of vinyl and matinees, of jeans and scarves, a world before panic. Peel back the music and slip in, eyes closed, heart poised. A grove of aspens stripped bare. A flash of gold in the winter sun. The missing ones.

Then a rock to my windshield like a shot to the chest. I shudder and shudder again. The sound of ice cracking under boots. It wakes my son. *Where are we?* he asks. Concentric circles like a stone dropped in water, cool and smooth to the touch. My death arrested. *Almost home,* I say. Almost home.

TEACHING MY CHILDREN TO TRESPASS

Hands to knees, knees to chest: commit.
Pass through wires that enclose, exclose,
look back on abandoned nest boxes,
a carnival of colour.

Prickly. No other way to describe this land, me,
this where I'm from: sagebrush, wild rose, hips
softening with the advance of seasons.
I am grassland. A complicated nose.

I carry the baby up and up to where my
legs burn, my mind clears
and my children's voices are satin ribbons
unfurling through the valley.

The trees, dead white and knobby-kneed,
a slash of colour across the tawny hills,
their golden shiver turned carpet of tears
on land that encloses, excloses.

Keep climbing. Trust the blind eye of gravity.
Paths emerge from a height.

NOTES

¶ **Prelude:** This poem began as a blessing I wrote on the occasion of a meal with poet Amanda Jernigan and photographer John Haney. *Yawp* is a reference to Walt Whitman's line "I sound my barbaric yawp over the roofs of the world," which appeared in the original edition of *Leaves of Grass* in 1855. ¶ **Correction Line:** A correction line is a uniquely western reminder of the curvature of the earth. The Dominion Land Survey divided western Canada into one-square-mile blocks. A square of 36 of these (6 miles by 6 miles) is a township, bounded on the north and south by range roads, and on the east and west by township roads. These township roads converge on the north pole, so every so often as one drives north or south, the road jogs to the east or west by a few dozen yards. Correction lines are at once banal and sublime, evidence of the enormity of the universe. ¶ **On Wilderness:** The epigraph is from Don McKay's *The Muskwa Assemblage* (Gaspereau Press, 2009). ¶ **Season Opener:** The *Ann Harvey* is the Canadian Coast Guard icebreaker. ¶ **St. Elmo's Fire:** St. Elmo's Fire is the weather phenomenon responsible for the bright blue ball of light sailors sometimes see at sea. It is also the name of a David Foster song I listened to incessantly, and completely without irony, during one formative summer in the eighties. ¶ **Running Errands:** This poem is inspired by Jan Zwicky's poem "Running Errands, Catching Sight of my Reflection," in *Forge* (Gaspereau Press, 2011). ¶ **The Rich in Airports:** The astute reader may notice a certain shared cadence here with various lists of Chuck Norris jokes that made the rounds late in the last century. ¶ **When in doubt,**

set it in Caslon: The epigraph from this poem (and its title) comes from an email I received from Dave Churchman, an Indianapolis-based letterpress printer. ¶ **Deluge:** On June 20, 2013, heavy rain triggered floods of rivers throughout central and southern Alberta: the Bow and Elbow Rivers in Calgary, the Sheep and Highwood Rivers south of Calgary, and the Red Deer River from Sundre through to Drumheller were affected. When all was said and done, 100,000 people were displaced, temporarily or less so, and Alberta was facing cleanup of Canada's costliest natural disaster. My family was one of the thousands temporarily displaced. Most of us passed the days and weeks following the flood in a kind of suspended animation, watching as more and more damage was revealed. These poems mark that time. ¶ **Intertriginous: Poems for Evolution:** February 12, 2009, marked Charles Darwin's 200th birthday, and the poems in this section were originally commissioned by Thaddeus Holownia to commemorate the occasion. The lines that title the poems are borrowed (more or less intact) from Darwin's *On the Origin of Species by Means of Natural Selection, or The Preservation of Favoured Races in the Struggle for Life* (London: W. Clowes & Sons, 1859): "Nature cares nothing for appearances ..." is for Merrill Francis; "Savages now sometimes cross their dogs with wild canine animals ..."is for Nick, whom I worked with while doing fieldwork on the Norwegian island of Spitsbergen in the summer of 1995; "We may console ourselves with the full belief that the war of nature is not incessant..." is for Colin, and the music, however brief; "Not one of our domestic animals can be named which has not in some country drooping ears ..." is for Chango, with apologies for the thunderstorms; "When

I view all beings not as special creations ..." is for Nature, finally winning over Nurture. ¶ **Other Kinds of Hungers:** The section epigraph comes from Richard Berlin's poem "Hospital Food" from *How JFK Killed My Father* (Pearl Editions, 2003) ¶ **Achilles:** Plantation owners would sometimes "hobble" slaves by slicing their Achilles tendons, limiting their ability of escape. ¶ **Fallen:** Based on a story once told to me about a man with latent osteomyelitis following a gunshot wound in WWII. The infection flared when he was much older, and it eventually took his life. The last two lines of the poem are what his family said about his death. ¶ **Badlands:** The epigraph comes from Patrick DeWitt's *The Sisters Brothers* (Anansi, 2011).

ACKNOWLEDGEMENTS

Thanks to Amanda Jernigan, Roberta Jackson, and Michael Crummey for your careful read of these poems. To my editor, publisher and letterpress provocateur, Andrew Steeves. And to my family, for the days. A big Labrador retriever kiss, from me to all of you.

INDEX OF POEM TITLES

The type used
in this book is LEO
designed by Patrick Griffin
(Toronto) and Hans van
Maanen (Amsterdam) and
issued by Canada Type in
January 2015. While based on
an archetypal Dutch skeleton,
it is a contemporary design,
robust enough for both offset
printing and pixels. It is issued
in three weights with (at the
request of Gaspereau Press)
optional long descenders for
use in typesetting books.

 ¶ Gaspereau Press acknowledges the support of the Canada Council for the Arts, the Department of Canadian Heritage (through the Canada Book Fund) and the Nova Scotia Department of Communities, Culture & Heritage.

This book was designed and typeset in Leo by Andrew Steeves and printed offset and bound under the direction of Gary Dunfield at Gaspereau Press Limited, Kentville, Nova Scotia.

1 2 3 4 5 6 7

LIBRARY AND ARCHIVES CANADA
CATALOGUING IN PUBLICATION

Kidd, Monica, 1972–, author
The year of our beautiful exile / Monica Kidd.

Poems.
ISBN 978-1-55447-143-0 (pbk.)

I. Title.

PS8571.I354Y43 2015 C811'.6 C2015-900707-0

GASPEREAU PRESS LIMITED ¶ GARY DUNFIELD
& ANDREW STEEVES ¶ PRINTERS & PUBLISHERS
47 Church Avenue, Kentville, Nova Scotia B4N 2M7
Literary Outfitters & Cultural Wilderness Guides